D0776820

HEALING PROMISES

JOSEPH PRINCE

CHARISMA
HOUSE

Most CHARISMA HOUSE BOOK GROUP products are available at special quantity discounts for bulk purchase for sales promotions, premiums, fund-raising, and educational needs. For details, write Charisma House Book Group, 600 Rinehart Road, Lake Mary, Florida 32746, or telephone (407) 333-0600.

HEALING PROMISES by Joseph Prince
Published by Charisma House
Charisma Media/Charisma House Book Group
600 Rinehart Road
Lake Mary, Florida 32746
www.charismahouse.com

Unless otherwise noted, all Scripture quotations are from the New King James Version of the Bible. Copyright © 1979, 1980, 1982 by Thomas Nelson, Inc., publishers. Used by permission.

Scripture quotations marked AMP are from the Amplified Bible. Old Testament copyright © 1965, 1987 by the Zondervan Corporation. The Amplified New Testament copyright © 1954, 1958, 1987 by the Lockman Foundation. Used by permission.

Scripture quotations marked KJV are from the King James Version of the Bible.

Scripture quotations marked NASB are from the New American Standard Bible, copyright © 1960, 1962, 1963, 1968, 1971, 1972, 1973, 1975, 1977, 1995 by The Lockman Foundation. Used by permission. (www.Lockman.org)

Scripture quotations marked NIV are from the Holy Bible, New International Version. Copyright © 1973, 1978, 1984, 2011 by Biblica, Inc. All rights reserved. Used by permission.

Visit the author's website at www.josephprince.com.

Library of Congress Control Number: 2012942666
International Standard Book Number: 978-1-62136-010-0

Published in association with: Joseph Prince Teaching Resources
www.josephprince.com

13 14 15 16 17 — 9 8 7 6 5 4
Printed in the United States of America

Contents

Introduction

Introduction

You are so precious and loved by God that He gave His only Son for you. Today, I want to encourage you to meditate on the finished work of our Lord Jesus and see His love and grace toward you.

Beloved, the more you focus on what Jesus has done for you at the cross, the more you'll experience His divine health in your body and wholeness in every part of your life.

I pray that as you immerse yourself in the healing promises in this book and see the Lord's love for you, you'll experience an abundance of His resurrection life—in your spirit, soul and body!

CHAPTER 1

God Wants You Healed

For God so loved the world that He gave His only begotten Son, that whoever believes in Him should not perish but have everlasting life. For God did not send His Son into the world to condemn the world, but that the world through Him might be saved.

—JOHN 3:16–17

But God showed his great love for us by sending Christ to die for us while we were still sinners.

—ROMANS 5:8, NLT

God *So* Loves You

Jesus was the apple of God's eye. He was God's darling Son, His infinite joy and delight.

Yet, God gave Jesus up for you. That's how much God loves you.

Just think about it: If you knew you could save a dying person by giving up something precious to you, would you go as far as to give up your only child whom you dearly love for that person?

Yet, that is exactly what God did to save you. Jesus, His beloved Son, died on the cross to cleanse you, heal you and redeem you—spirit, soul and body! That is how precious you are to God!

He who did not spare His own Son, but delivered Him up for us all, how shall He not with Him also freely give us all things?

—ROMANS 8:32

Your Healing Is Part Of The Deal

Once you realize how very much God loves Jesus, His darling Son, ask yourself this: If God *willingly* gave Jesus up for me, would He withhold healing from me?

If God withholds your healing after He has already given you Jesus, then it would mean that your healing is greater or more important than Jesus.

No my friend, He has *already* given you heaven's best. How will He not also **freely** give you all things, including the healing and wholeness you desire?

If **GOD**
did not withhold
heaven's best
(JESUS)
from you…

...He *will not withhold*
healing
from you.

Surely He has borne our griefs (sicknesses, weaknesses, and distresses) and carried our sorrows and pains [of punishment], yet we [ignorantly] considered Him stricken, smitten, and afflicted by God [as if with leprosy]. But He was wounded for our transgressions, He was bruised for our guilt and iniquities; the chastisement [needful to obtain] peace and well-being for us was upon Him, and with the stripes [that wounded] Him we are healed and made whole.

—Isaiah 53:4–5, AMP

By His Stripes You Are Healed!

Isaiah 53 is proof forevermore of the Lord's love for you and His desire for you to be whole. How important is your healing and health to Him? It's so important that Jesus Himself paid the heavy and terrible price for your wholeness.

When Mel Gibson's *The Passion Of The Christ* was released, people complained that the scourging scene was too graphic and violent. The truth is that it portrayed only a fraction of what our Lord really suffered on our behalf.

Jesus was violently scourged beyond human recognition by the Roman torture equipment. His flesh was shredded to the point His bones were exposed, starkly white amidst the blood and torn muscles.

He bore the stripes so that we don't have to. His body was broken so that ours can be whole. And by His stripes, we have been healed!

———— ❧ ————

*...On the night when he was betrayed, the Lord
Jesus took some bread and gave thanks to God
for it. Then he broke it in pieces and said, "This
is my body, which is given for you. Do this to
remember me." In the same way, he took the
cup of wine after supper, saying, "This cup is the
new covenant between God and his people—an
agreement confirmed with my blood. Do this to
remember me as often as you drink it."*

—**1 Corinthians 11:23–25, NLT**

Partake Your Way To Wholeness

When you remember how Jesus willingly came to save you and suffered for your healing at the cross, it will cast out every fear of not receiving healing from Him.

That's what partaking of the Holy Communion is about. When you hold the bread in your hand, simply remember how Jesus' body was broken at the cross so that yours may be healed and whole. Say, "Lord Jesus, thank You for bearing my condition on Your own body at the cross. When the lashes fell across Your back, my condition died. It has no right to linger in my body!"

Likewise, when you partake of the cup, remember that Jesus shed His blood to save you. Say, "Jesus, thank You for Your shed blood that has washed away my sins and made me righteous. Because I am righteous in Your sight, healing belongs to me. I receive Your healing and resurrection life for my body right now."

Beloved, remember the Lord and partake your way to divine health!

*Suddenly, a man with leprosy approached
him and knelt before him. "Lord," the man
said, "if you are willing, you can heal me
and make me clean." Jesus reached out and
touched him. "I am willing," he said.
"Be healed!" And instantly the
leprosy disappeared.*

—**Matthew 8:2–3**, NLT

*"I will give you back your health and heal
your wounds," says the Lord.*

—**Jeremiah 30:17**, NLT

God Is Able And *Willing* To Heal You

Once, there was a leper who came to Jesus saying, "Lord, if You are willing, You can make me clean." This man didn't have a problem believing that Jesus had the ability and power to heal him. He just wasn't sure if Jesus was *willing* to do it for him.

I want you to look at Jesus' response to the leper and see God's heart for you where healing is concerned. Jesus answered the leper by touching him and saying, "I am willing. Be healed."

What did Jesus say? **"I am willing."** Did He just say it and do nothing? No, He stretched forth His hand to the leper and restored the afflicted man to wholeness.

Today, God wants you to know that He is both able AND willing to heal you. Start to realize and believe that He wants you healed more than you want to be healed!

"I AM *ABLE*...

"...I AM also *WILLING*."

—Jesus

Do not fear, little flock, for it is your Father's good pleasure to give you the kingdom.

—**LUKE 12:32**

If you then, being evil, know how to give good gifts to your children, how much more will your Father who is in heaven give good things to those who ask Him!

—**MATTHEW 7:11**

God Is Your Loving Father

God wants you to know that He is not the kind of Father who wants you sick and defeated. Instead, He is the kind of Father who enjoys providing for your needs. He is a good Father who will not withhold healing and a healthy body from you.

As your loving Father, God's joy is to see you blessed with the best. If you, in spite of your faults, know how to give good gifts to your children, how much more will your Father in heaven give good things to you when you ask Him!

My prayer today is that you will know just how much your Father loves you and be bold to ask Him for what you need.

"Lord, help!" they cried in their trouble, and he saved them from their distress. He sent out his word and healed them, snatching them from the door of death.

—PSALM 107:19–20, NLT

He has delivered us from the power of darkness and conveyed us into the kingdom of the Son of His love, in whom we have redemption through His blood, the forgiveness of sins.

—COLOSSIANS 1:13–14

Your Redeemer Has Delivered You From All Sicknesses

Jesus willingly came down from heaven to redeem you from a life of sickness, poverty and death to a life of freedom, health and blessings! He willingly suffered for you at the cross so that you may walk in the fullness of redemption's blessings—divine health, restoration, peace and provision!

Simply look to Jesus and His finished work today and see how much God loves you. You will see how much more God wants to bless you than you want to be blessed, and how much more He wants to heal you than you want to be well!

For I am persuaded that neither death nor life, nor angels nor principalities nor powers, nor things present nor things to come, nor height nor depth, nor any other created thing, shall be able to separate us from the love of God which is in Christ Jesus our Lord.

—ROMANS 8:38–39

Beloved, I pray that in all respects you may prosper and be in good health, just as your soul prospers.

—3 JOHN 1:2, NASB

God Wants You To Always Prosper And Be In Health

The Bible tells us that God's love is so immeasurable, powerful and all-encompassing that nothing can ever separate us from it.

Because God loves you so much, His desire above all things is always for you, His beloved child, to prosper in all that you do and **be in health**, even as your soul prospers.

If an earthly father would want his child to be happy and healthy, how much more God, your heavenly Father? He wants you well and He is willing to use His power to make you well!

For I know the thoughts that I think toward you,
says the Lord, thoughts of peace and not of evil,
to give you a future and a hope.

—JEREMIAH 29:11

…the very hairs on your head are all numbered.
So don't be afraid; you are more valuable to God
than a whole flock of sparrows.

—LUKE 12:7, NLT

If It Troubles You, God Wants To Take Care Of It!

Many Christians make the mistake of thinking that God is too busy taking care of the "big things" to be interested in the little problems they are facing.

But God is not like that. He is not just God Almighty, He is also your heavenly Father who loves you! To God, whether it's a new pimple on your face, a sore throat or an aching back, no matter how trivial or commonplace it sounds, if it troubles you, He wants to take care of it!

If, as the Bible says, God bothers to keep track of how many hairs you have on your head, then there is no symptom, no discomfort and no condition in your body that He doesn't know of or care about. His love for you is all-encompassing, personal and in-depth. There is nothing in your body or life too small that you can't bring to Him and watch Him take care of!

…I have loved you with an everlasting love…

—JEREMIAH 31:3

*Since you are precious and honored in my sight,
and because I love you… Do not be afraid,
for I am with you…*

—ISAIAH 43:4–5, NIV

*…He cares for you affectionately and cares
about you watchfully.*

—1 PETER 5:7, AMP

"I have loved you with an **everlasting love** because *you are precious to Me.* Do not be afraid."

—Jesus

Then they came to the other side of the sea, to the country of the Gadarenes. And when He had come out of the boat, immediately there met Him out of the tombs a man with an unclean spirit…For He [Jesus] said to him, "Come out of the man, unclean spirit!"

—Mark 5:1–2, 8

For I have come down from heaven, not to do My own will, but the will of Him who sent Me…And this is the will of Him who sent Me, that everyone who sees the Son and believes in Him may have everlasting life…

—John 6:38, 40

He Has Gone The Distance To Heal You

The Gadarene demoniac was someone who was isolated, left alone and shunned by people. He had no one to turn to. People were afraid of him and there was no one who could heal his condition—until Jesus came.

Jesus crossed the entire lake of Galilee just to heal this man, despite the devil trying to stop Him with a storm. He travelled a great distance just to minister healing to that man and set him free. That's the kind of loving Savior He is!

Just as Jesus went a long way to heal one man, He went to great lengths, to the point of death, to purchase liberty, blessings and health for you. No sickness or circumstance, however grave or disastrous, is greater than what He has already done for you!

Since the children have flesh and blood, he too shared in their humanity so that by his death he might destroy him who holds the power of death—that is, the devil—and free those who all their lives were held in slavery by their fear of death.

—HEBREWS 2:14–15, NIV

The thief does not come except to steal, and to kill, and to destroy. I have come that they may have life, and that they may have it more abundantly.

—JOHN 10:10

Rescued From Death

God never meant for man to die. God counts death as an enemy. He hates death. All things that lead to death—all forms of sickness and disease— are not from God. Jesus wept at Lazarus' tomb because He remembered that it was never God's heart for man to fall sick, grow old and die.

But because the consequence of sin is death, God sent Jesus to bear the punishment for all our sins. And at the cross, Jesus conquered death once and for all, setting us free from sicknesses and diseases forever!

Today, God's heart is for you to be healed and whole. He loves you so much that He sent Jesus to redeem you from death. The cross of Jesus is the reason you can enjoy His divine health, peace and abundant life today!

*The Lord shall preserve you from all evil;
He shall preserve your soul. The Lord
shall preserve your going out and your
coming in from this time forth,
and even forevermore.*

—PSALM 121:7–8

*In this the love of God was manifested
toward us, that God has sent His only
begotten Son into the world, that we
might live through Him.*

—1 JOHN 4:9

The Divine Exchange Has Set You Free

Jesus wore the crown of thorns on His head so that you can have a sound mind free from fears, guilt, depression, anxieties and stress.

Jesus' feet brought Him to places where there was lack, diseases, condemnation and even death. At the cross, those feet were nail-pierced so that you do not need to be in such places yourself. He has rescued you from having to accept and suffer these things in life.

Jesus didn't have to. He chose to. Why? Because He loves you. He spared not even Himself so that you may have every blessing of health, wholeness and abundant life!

*…I will set apart the land of Goshen, in which My
people dwell, that no swarms of flies shall be there, in
order that you may know that I am the Lord in the
midst of the land. I will make a difference between
My people and your people…*

—Exodus 8:22–23

*A thousand may fall at your side, and ten thousand at
your right hand; but it shall not come near you.*

—Psalm 91:7

*Now I am no longer in the world, but these are in the
world, and I come to You. Holy Father, keep through
Your name those whom You have given Me, that they
may be one as We are… They are not of the world,
just as I am not of the world.*

—John 17:11, 16

Protected In The Secret Place Of The Most High

When there were plagues and pestilences all over ancient Egypt because Pharaoh refused to let God's people go, look at what God said about the children of Israel: "…I will set apart the land of Goshen, in which My people dwell…I will make a difference between My people and your people…" The Bible records that although Egypt was plagued by swarms of flies and other pestilences, the Israelites were safe in Goshen, completely untouched by the troubles!

Don't be afraid when you hear or read of terrible diseases in the world. As God's beloved child, you are in the world, but not *of* the world. And as the children of Israel were kept safe and protected in Goshen, so will the Lord keep you safe in the secret place of the Most High.

Do not be afraid of the terrors of the night, nor the arrow that flies in the day. Do not dread the disease that stalks in darkness, nor the disaster that strikes at midday. Though a thousand fall at your side, though ten thousand are dying around you, these evils will not touch you.

—**PSALM 91:5–7,** NLT

DO NOT
BE AFRAID.
There is NO disease
or terror that
JESUS
has not taken on and
**DEFEATED FOR
YOU.**

For you did not receive a spirit that makes you a slave again to fear, but you received the Spirit of sonship. And by him we cry, "Abba, Father."

—ROMANS 8:15, NIV

There is no fear in love; but perfect love casts out fear, because fear involves torment. But he who fears has not been made perfect in love.

—1 JOHN 4:18

His Perfect Love Drives Out Every Fear

If you think that God is mad at you or that He is out to punish you, how can you have faith that He hears your prayer for healing? How can you believe Him for your miracle?

Yet, the truth is that God loves you so much that He gave you Jesus, heaven's best, so that you will NEVER be cut-off from Him no matter what you've done or not done. Jesus went to the cross for you so that God will always be with you and for you, to heal you and do **good** to you.

When you have a deep revelation of how much God loves you, you can't remain sick for long. You won't be afraid that He may be keeping His healing power from you. Keep feeding on His perfect love for you. Keep meditating on it. It's the sure antidote to fear!

*For even the Son of Man did not come to be
served, but to serve, and to give His life
a ransom for many.*

—MARK 10:45

*When the sun was setting, all those who had any
that were sick with various diseases brought them
to Him; and He laid His hands on every one of
them and healed them.*

—LUKE 4:40

God Wants You To Draw From Him

Did you know that *giving* to you actually brings joy to God's heart? When you place a demand on Him—like look to Him to heal you—you let Him be God. When you draw from His fullness— His abundance of life, health and blessing—you delight Him!

That's why God wants you to come expectantly to Him for your healing today. See Him ready to pour His abundance out for you. See Him rejoicing when you call upon Him. As you see His heart of love that always wants to give to you, you will see your healing manifest!

Jesus replied, "If you only knew the gift God has for you and who you are speaking to, you would ask me, and I would give you living water ... But those who drink the water I give will never be thirsty again. It becomes a fresh, bubbling spring within them, giving them eternal life."

—**JOHN 4:10, 14, NLT**

For the Lord God is a sun and shield; the Lord will give grace and glory; no good thing will He withhold from those who walk uprightly.

—**PSALM 84:11**

God Wants To Pour Healing Into You

Come to God for your healing. Don't hesitate. God, who is so full of goodness and supply, is always willing to bless, preserve, heal and restore you.

Jesus was physically weary when He ministered to the Samaritan woman at the well. Yet, He invited her to draw from Him the living water that would never run dry. When she went away, full in her heart and rejoicing, *He* was strengthened, refreshed and rejuvenated!

Beloved, when you come empty and draw from God, the One who has endless supply, you honor Him and let Him be God. You free Him to pour His abundant supply of health, wholeness and peace into your life!

A woman in the crowd had suffered for twelve years with constant bleeding. She had suffered a great deal from many doctors, and over the years she had spent everything she had to pay them, but she had gotten no better. In fact, she had gotten worse. She had heard about Jesus, so she came up behind him through the crowd and touched his robe. For she thought to herself, "If I can just touch his robe, I will be healed." Immediately the bleeding stopped, and she could feel in her body that she had been healed of her terrible condition.

—MARK 5:25–29, NLT

Hear How God Is Always Good Toward The Sick

She had been hemorrhaging continuously for 12 years. Medical science had no answer. Money to pay for expensive medication had run dry, very likely with all faith and hope that she could be made well.

And then one day, she heard of a travelling preacher, teacher and healer. She heard about His compassionate touch, His kind eyes and healing hands. She heard that everyone who came to Him to be healed was healed. Suddenly, faith to believe that she would be next sparked on the inside. And when this woman touched Jesus with that faith, power left His body and healed her instantly!

What had fired up her faith? It was simply hearing about how good, kind and loving Jesus was that led her to believe that He was both able and willing to heal her.

God is just as willing to heal you today. Just focus on His love for you. See His heart to heal you of your condition and faith will ignite in you, sparking off an explosion of healing in your body!

"So don't worry about these things, saying,
'What will we eat? What will we drink?
What will we wear?' These things dominate
the thoughts of unbelievers, but your
heavenly Father already knows
all your needs … and he will
give you everything you need."

—**MATTHEW 6:31–33, NLT**

Every good gift and every perfect gift is from
above, and comes down from the Father of lights,
with whom there is no variation
or shadow of turning.

—**JAMES 1:17**

Your Heavenly Father Wants You Blessed And Healthy!

If you were a parent, wouldn't you want the best for your children? Would you ever want them to be diseased, poor and suffering? Of course not. You'd want your children to be blessed, strong and healthy, and enjoying the best things in life, wouldn't you?

Think about this for a moment. If you on earth know how to give good gifts to your children, how much more your Father in heaven who loves you and knows how to bless you and your children with divine health, provision and protection!

Beloved, expect to receive good from the Lord, who is full of grace and mercy, every day!

What then shall we say to these things?
If God is for us, who can be against us?
—ROMANS 8:31

Who shall separate us from the love of Christ?
Shall tribulation, or distress, or persecution,
or famine, or nakedness, or peril, or sword?
—ROMANS 8:35

Yet in all these things we are more than
conquerors through Him who loved us.
—ROMANS 8:37

If God Is For You, Who Can Be Against You?

When the Almighty God is your loving Father and you are His beloved, what fears can you have? Fear of the future? Fear of sickness? Fear of death?

Beloved, when you have a revelation of how much God loves you and that He sees you completely righteous by the blood of Jesus Christ, all your fears will dissipate, for if God is for you, who or what can be against you? What sickness can come against you and successfully bring you down?

So look away from your circumstances and call out without fear to your Father. He loves you and will never condemn you! Feed on His everlasting love for you and receive your healing from Him!

If **GOD** *is*
FOR YOU
and not against you…

...then He *is* for *your healing and* against *the disease.* How then can the disease prevail against you?

*A funeral procession was coming out as he approached
the village gate. The young man who
had died was a widow's only son… When the Lord
saw her, his heart overflowed with compassion. "Don't
cry!" he said. Then he walked over to the coffin and
touched it, and the bearers stopped.
"Young man," he said, "I tell you, get up."
Then the dead boy sat up and began to talk!
And Jesus gave him back to his mother.*

—LUKE 7:12–15, NLT

He Is Moved With Compassion For You

There's a story of Jesus ministering to a widow at Nain when He saw the dead body of her only son being carried out of the city gate to be buried. Overflowing with compassion, He reached out to her and said, "Don't cry."

Rather than extend more condemnation and confusion to the widow, He extended His compassion and brought the young man back to life. Our Lord Jesus, the same yesterday, today and forever, also comes to you when you are most distraught and says, "Don't cry." His love for you will move Him to give you the miracle you need.

Even if the doctor has given you a negative report, trust His compassion for you. He will breathe His life into every situation of sickness and death until you see His resurrection life manifest!

Beloved, I pray that you may prosper in all things and be in health, just as your soul prospers.

—3 JOHN 1:2

When evening had come, they brought to Him many who were demon-possessed. And He cast out the spirits with a word, and healed all who were sick, that it might be fulfilled which was spoken by Isaiah the prophet, saying: "He Himself took our infirmities and bore our sicknesses."

—MATTHEW 8:16–17

God's Perfect Will Is For You To Be Healed

Look no further than 3 John 1:2 for a prayer that reflects God's heart. That's how you know that He wants you healed, healthy and never sick, as much as He wants your soul to prosper!

Don't go by human experiences to know if God wants His people healed today. If you say, "Well, I know of Christians who are sick," I can point you to many others whom God has healed. We're not called to base our believing on human experiences. We're called to believe God's Word.

Beloved, never put your eyes on people and their experiences, even good ones. The basis of your faith must always be God's Word. Believe that God still heals today because His Word says so!

Place experience above GOD'S WORD *and you'll become* *shakable.*

Place
GOD'S WORD
above experience,
and you'll become
UNSHAKABLE,
heart, mind and body.

CHAPTER 2

Jesus Is Your Healer

... *when they came to Marah, they*
could not drink the waters of Marah,
for they were bitter... And the people
complained against Moses, saying, "What
shall we drink?" So he cried out to the
Lord, and the Lord showed him a tree.
When he cast it into the waters, the waters
were made sweet.

—EXODUS 15:23–25

Always Bring In The Cross

I love the story of how God turned bitter, poisonous waters into sweet, refreshing waters for His people when they came to a place called Marah (meaning "bitterness" in Hebrew). When the Israelites could not drink the water, Moses cried out to the Lord. The Lord showed him a tree, which Moses cast into the waters. When he did that, the Bible says that "the waters were made sweet."

I love how God's solution then is still God's solution now: Throw in the tree—a picture of Jesus at the cross—to turn the bitter waters sweet.

Today, in the midst of the bitter waters of your pain or condition, I want to encourage you to bring in Jesus and see what He did for you at the cross. Relief and healing don't come from dwelling on your pain. Bring in the tree—the cross of Jesus— and see your bitter waters become sweet!

And Jesus went about all Galilee, teaching in their synagogues, preaching the gospel of the kingdom, and healing all kinds of sickness and all kinds of disease among the people.

—MATTHEW 4:23

And the whole multitude sought to touch Him, for power went out from Him and healed them all.

—LUKE 6:19

Everyone Who Came To Jesus Was Healed

Did you know that when Jesus walked on earth, more than two-thirds of His ministry involved healing the sick? He went about healing the sick and all who came to Him were healed. The Bible records that "the whole multitude sought to touch Him, for power went out from Him and **healed them all**."

I wish that somebody in Hollywood would produce that scene in Luke 6:19. You see the sick, lame and blind coming to Jesus. And every time one of them touches Him, BAM! His healing virtue is powerfully released and the person is healed and overjoyed! That's a powerful image to have in your mind whenever you are believing God for healing!

*News about him spread as far as Syria,
and people soon began bringing to
him all who were sick. And whatever
their sickness or disease, or if they
were demon-possessed or epileptic or
paralyzed—he healed them all.*

—**MATTHEW 4:24, NLT**

…I am the Lord who heals you.

—**EXODUS 15:26**

See The Real Jesus

The Bible tells us that if you want to know what God is like, just look at Jesus! If you want to know how the Father feels about healing the sick, just look at Jesus! Jesus ALWAYS healed the sick who came to him. The blind, lame, mute, deaf and demon-possessed—He healed them ALL!

Jesus NEVER gave sickness to anybody. You'll find Jesus healing lepers when He was on earth, but you'll never find Him calling anyone over and saying to the person, "You are too healthy and good-looking. Receive some leprosy to learn how to be humble!" No, when a leper came to Him, uncertain that Jesus would want to heal him, Jesus, full of compassion, told him firmly, "I am WILLING. Be healed!"

That's your Jesus. That is your God. He is the Lord who heals you—today and always!

*… God anointed Jesus of Nazareth
with the Holy Spirit and with
power, who went about doing good
and healing all who were oppressed
by the devil, for God was with Him.*

—ACTS 10:38

*Jesus Christ is the same yesterday,
today, and forever.*

—HEBREWS 13:8

He Is Still The Same

Jesus had prioritized divine healing during His earthly ministry. The Bible tells us that He went about "doing good and healing **all** who were oppressed by the devil." In fact, **anyone** and **everyone** who came to Him for healing—whether it was for their children, servants, friends or for themselves—received their healing. Not a single one who had come to Him went away without receiving healing from Him.

And Jesus, who is "the same yesterday, today, and forever," will do the same for you today. His heart still beats with compassion for you. He will never miss an opportunity to do good to you—to heal you of your broken body, emotional scars and weary spirit—and to bless you!

For I am the Lord, I do not change…
—**MALACHI 3:6**

But you are always the same;
you will live forever.
—**PSALM 102:27, NLT**

And Jesus said to him, "I will come
and heal him."
—**MATTHEW 8:7**

He has *never changed.*
Ever constant,
ever compassionate,
JESUS *STILL HEALS*
YOU *TODAY*.

No one living in Zion will say,
"I am ill"; and the sins of those who
dwell there will be forgiven.

—Isaiah 33:24, NIV

But he was pierced for our rebellion,
crushed for our sins. He was beaten so
we could be whole. He was whipped so
we could be healed.

—Isaiah 53:5, NLT

Both Forgiveness And Healing Are Yours

God loves you so much that He not only caused Jesus to carry your sins, but also your diseases at the cross. Your forgiveness and healing are BOTH part of Jesus' finished work at Calvary. He was crushed for your sins, and He was also lashed, scourged and whipped for your healing!

My friend, God has already healed you of all your diseases, afflictions and pains at the cross. You might have heard it taught that healing is a "bonus blessing" because it's over and on top of salvation. But nothing could be further from the truth. Your salvation, purchased by Jesus at the cross, **includes healing**. Today, because of the cross of Jesus, you have the right to COMPLETE WHOLENESS, both within and without!

Give thanks to the Lord, for he is good!
His faithful love endures forever.

—1 CHRONICLES 16:34, NLT

We know how much God loves us, and
we have put our trust in his love.

—1 JOHN 4:16, NLT

The thief does not come except to steal,
and to kill, and to destroy. I have come
that they may have life, and that they
may have it more abundantly.

—JOHN 10:10

God Is Not Out To Destroy You

The Bible tells us clearly that God is a God of love, and our God of love is a good God! He is a God who longs to do good to His people. In fact, God desires to load His children with benefits every day!

My friend, don't ever be mistaken that a good God will give you sicknesses, diseases and all sorts of physical afflictions. God is constant and constantly good. Sicknesses, on the other hand, are always bad. They are part of the curse. Their purpose is to destroy a person.

Our good God gave us His Son, Jesus, so that you may not be destroyed but have LIFE, and have it MORE ABUNDANTLY! The Lord does not take away your life. Instead, He gives, multiplies and restores to you life and health!

*And the Lord will take away from you all
sickness, and none of the evil diseases of Egypt
which you knew will He put upon you…*
—DEUTERONOMY 7:15, AMP

*…In the last days, they will tremble in awe of
the Lord and of his goodness.*
—HOSEA 3:5, NLT

God Is A Good Father

Stop believing the LIE that God gives you sicknesses, diseases and accidents to punish you or teach you a lesson. These things are from the devil, and because of Jesus' finished work, we have been redeemed from every evil work and curse. We can receive protection from every evil occurrence, sickness and disease. And by the stripes on Jesus' back, we are healed!

Don't fight for the right to be sick and defeated when God is full of grace and mercy, and wants you to be healthy, blessed and protected from all evil occurrences! Start to expect good gifts from the Lord. Reject anything that even remotely suggests God is angry with you, and disciplines you with sicknesses and accidents. He is a good God and a good father!

True or false?

God gives people sicknesses.

Answer: False

True or false?

God is a good God and a good Father.

Answer: True

*Surely He shall deliver you from
the snare of the fowler and from
the perilous pestilence.*

—PSALM 91:3

*With long life I will satisfy him,
and show him My salvation.*

—PSALM 91:16

God Satisfies You With Long Life

God's heart is never for you to die prematurely, nor to live a life that is miserable. Psalm 91:16 says, "With long life I will satisfy him, and show him My salvation."

This means that God not only wants you to have a long life, but He also wants you to have a *satisfying* life that is full of His peace, provision and joy! In the verse, the word "salvation" is the Hebrew word *Yeshua*, the name of Jesus. So God will satisfy you with a long life that is full of Jesus and His grace!

Chronic illness, depression or a short life is not, and will never be, part of God's plan for you. He wants you to experience a long, full life in which you walk in all the blessings of health, wholeness and provision that He has given you through Jesus!

*...the soldiers twisted a crown of thorns
and put it on His head...*

—JOHN 19:2

*The Lord shall preserve you from all evil;
He shall preserve your soul. The Lord
shall preserve your going out and your
coming in from this time forth,
and even forevermore.*

—PSALM 121:7–8

*...Do not be afraid...for I will protect
you, and your reward will be great.*

—GENESIS 15:1, NLT

Your Mind Matters To Him

Doctors tell us that many of the sicknesses we suffer in our bodies are *psychosomatic*—they are a result of mental or emotional stress we have put ourselves under.

Perhaps you were abused or emotionally hurt by someone you trusted. Maybe you still feel angry and hurt when you think about it. Beloved, I want to encourage you to start involving Jesus. He is your answer. See the Lord holding you, gently healing your wounds. See Him restoring you, putting courage into your heart and taking away every sense of shame and guilt.

At the cross, Jesus took on Himself the bitter sting of every one of your frustrations, hurts and emotional pains when He wore the crown of thorns on your behalf. He did it so that you can be free from fears, depression and stress, and enjoy His peace and rest in your heart, mind and body.

The Lord is my shepherd; I have all that I need. He lets me rest in green meadows; he leads me beside peaceful streams. He renews my strength. He guides me along right paths, bringing honor to his name.

—PSALM 23:1–3, NLT

I am the good shepherd. The good shepherd gives His life for the sheep.

—JOHN 10:11

Jesus Is Your Good Shepherd

When I was a young believer, I heard a preacher say, "In order to draw a straying lamb to him, a shepherd will break its legs. When it's unable to walk, he will nurse the lamb back to health. Once it's healthy again, the lamb will be attached to him." That terrifying picture of a shepherd stuck in my head for years!

One day, I was able to ask a real shepherd if that story was true. Aghast, he replied, "That's nonsense! What kind of shepherd does that?"

Sadly, there are people today who still believe this nonsense. Beloved, Jesus is our **good** shepherd. When He is your shepherd, you will not want for *anything*. He is your supply of everything you need. He does not "break your legs." Instead, He leads you to places of rest, refreshing, healing and renewal of strength!

*God…shares with us the life of his Son
and our Master Jesus. He will never give
up on you. Never forget that.*

—*1 CORINTHIANS 1:9, THE MESSAGE*

*Giving thanks to the Father who has
qualified us to be partakers of the
inheritance of the saints in the light.*

—*COLOSSIANS 1:12*

*Everyone was trying to touch him—
so much energy surging from him,
so many people healed!*

—*LUKE 6:19, THE MESSAGE*

Partners And Partakers

Make no mistake: Jesus is the purest form of life, and He's called us to share intimately with Him this incredible God-kind of life. It's a life where sicknesses and diseases have NO PLACE. And when you became a born-again believer, God qualified you to partake of this life.

In the face of your symptoms, in the midst of your fears and worries, see yourself—spirit, soul and body—immersed and surrounded by the very life that fills our Lord Jesus. It will swallow up every symptom of pain, weakness and death until you are walking in its fullness!

*Jesus stopped and said, "Call him."
So they called to the blind man,
"Cheer up! On your feet! He's calling
you." Throwing his cloak aside, he
jumped to his feet and came to Jesus.
"What do you want me to do for
you?" Jesus asked him. The blind man
said, "Rabbi, I want to see." "Go," said
Jesus, "your faith has healed you."
Immediately he received his sight and
followed Jesus along the road.*

—**MARK 10:49–52**, NIV

Your Need Is Your Qualification

Bartimaeus was a blind beggar at the gate of Jericho. Talk about being insignificant. Not only was he just another beggar in a place probably swarming with them, he didn't even have a real name—"Bartimaeus" merely means "son of Timaeus"!

And yet Jesus, the King of heaven and the incarnate Son of God, stopped in His tracks when this blind, nameless and often-ignored beggar called out to Him. Jesus heard him and had compassion on him, and responded to his need. He treated Bartimaeus with respect, empathized with the desire of his heart and set him free to see again.

Like Bartimaeus, **your need is your qualification for His miracle.** And when it comes to your need, it is NEVER too insignificant to Jesus!

Then great multitudes came to Him,
having with them the lame, blind,
mute, maimed, and many others;
and they laid them down at
Jesus' feet, and He healed them.
—**MATTHEW 15:30**

Jesus had compassion on them and
touched their eyes. Immediately they
received their sight and followed him.
—**MATTHEW 20:34, NIV**

All you need to do
for God to heal you is to
come to Him
with your need.

And behold, there was a woman who had a spirit of infirmity eighteen years, and was bent over and could in no way raise herself up. But when Jesus saw her, He called her to Him and said to her, "Woman, you are loosed from your infirmity." And He laid His hands on her, and immediately she was made straight, and glorified God.

—*LUKE 13:11–13*

Now may the Lord's strength be displayed, just as you have declared…

—*NUMBERS 14:17, NIV*

You Are Set Free From The Curse!

One of my favorite stories is of Jesus healing a woman bowed over with a spirit of infirmity for 18 years. Imagine never being able to see the sky or rainbows, but only the dust of the earth and the grubby feet of people—what a painful existence!

I love how Jesus saw her and immediately called her over to receive a miracle from Him. The woman had been bound in this condition for 18 years, a number which represents bondage in the Bible. When Jesus said to her, "Woman, you are loosed from your infirmity," He was proclaiming liberty over her and setting her free from the bondage of the devil. He laid hands on her and she immediately received her healing.

Today, you have already been set free from the curse of disease by Jesus' one perfect sacrifice at the cross. Proclaim your liberty won by His finished work!

*One of the men lying there had been sick for
thirty-eight years. When Jesus saw him and
knew he had been ill for a long time, he asked
him, "Would you like to get well?" "I can't, sir,"
the sick man said, "for I have no one to put
me into the pool when the water bubbles up.
Someone else always gets there ahead of me."
Jesus told him, "Stand up, pick up your mat,
and walk!" Instantly, the man was healed! He
rolled up his sleeping mat and began walking…*

—**JOHN 5:5–9**, NLT

*God is our refuge and strength,
a very present help in trouble.*

—**PSALM 46:1**

He Is All You Need

A man, paralyzed for 38 years, lay by the pool of Bethesda, waiting for an angel to come to stir its waters—it was known that the first one to step into the waters then would be healed of his condition. But because of his paralysis, the man could never be the first one in. So he kept waiting there, hoping for a miracle.

Then one day, he encountered a Man higher than angels—Jesus—who met him at the point of his need. Jesus came to the paralyzed man, and this man, who had been suffering for so many years, walked away completely healed.

Today, Jesus wants to meet you at the point of your need. *You don't need special seasons, circumstances or angels to see the manifestation of your healing.* You only need the Lord, who is here right now to heal you. He is your very present help in time of need!

I am still confident of this: I will see the goodness of the Lord in the land of the living.

—**PSALM 27:13**, NIV

Oh, give thanks to the Lord, for He is good! For His mercy endures forever.

—**PSALM 118:1**

The Lord is my strength and song, and He has become my salvation.

—**PSALM 118:14**

His Goodness Is Your Solution

In the midst of feelings and physical symptoms that can change from day to day, two things remain constant: The Lord is good, and He wants to be good to you!

Today, however bad things may be in your body or life, you can say with the psalmist:

> *I am still confident of this: I will see the goodness of the Lord in the land of the living.*

Whatever physical challenge you are facing, the Lord's goodness will come to your rescue!

CHAPTER 3

Freely Receive Your Healing

Some people brought to him a paralyzed man on a mat. Seeing their faith, Jesus said to the paralyzed man, "Be encouraged, my child! Your sins are forgiven."

—MATTHEW 9:2, NLT

"...I will prove to you that the Son of Man has the authority on earth to forgive sins." Then Jesus turned to the paralyzed man and said, "Stand up, pick up your mat, and go home!" And the man jumped up and went home!

—MATTHEW 9:6–7, NLT

Beloved, I wish above all things that thou mayest prosper and be in health, even as thy soul prospereth.

—3 JOHN 1:2, KJV

'Your Sins Are Forgiven!'

Undeterred by the crowds blocking their way, four good friends broke through the roof of the house Jesus was in and lowered their paralyzed friend on his mat, right in front of Jesus. When Jesus saw the sick man, He said, "Be encouraged, My child! Your sins are forgiven."

These bold, gracious words scandalized some legalistic scribes there, but they penetrated and restored the soul of the poor paralytic. For years, he had probably believed that he was paralyzed because of his sins. Jesus said to the man, "Stand up, pick up your mat, and go home!" And the paralytic man **leaped to his feet**!

Pay attention to this: Before the man could receive healing from the Lord, he needed to be assured that his sins were forgiven. I want you to know right now that YOUR SINS ARE FORGIVEN because you believe in Jesus!

I write to you, little children, because your sins are forgiven you for His name's sake.

—1 JOHN 2:12

He has delivered us from the power of darkness and conveyed us into the kingdom of the Son of His love, in whom we have redemption through His blood, the forgiveness of sins.

—COLOSSIANS 1:13–14

A Righteous Foundation For Your Forgiveness

It is because of JESUS that your sins are forgiven. At the cross, He bore your sins and was punished to the full by the fiery wrath of God. He did a *perfect* work of removing your sins once and for all, that's why He could cry out, "IT IS FINISHED!"

Beloved, the wall of sin that once stood between you and God has been broken down by the finished work of Jesus. His blood shed at Calvary has washed away your sins and released the flood tide of God's blessings.

Today, you have a righteous and rock-solid foundation for your forgiveness and healing— Jesus and His finished work!

*In Him we have redemption
through His blood, the forgiveness
of sins, according to the
riches of His grace.*

—EPHESIANS 1:7

God's grace
knows no bounds.

You are forgiven
according
to the riches of
His grace!

*...God made you alive with Christ,
for he forgave all our sins.*

—COLOSSIANS 2:13, NLT

*Unlike those other high priests, he does not need
to offer sacrifices every day. They did this for
their own sins first and then for the sins of the
people. But Jesus did this once for all when he
offered himself as the sacrifice
for the people's sins.*

—HEBREWS 7:27, NLT

*When he died, he died once to break
the power of sin. But now that he lives,
he lives for the glory of God.*

—ROMANS 6:10, NLT

All Is Forgiven, Once For All

My friend, here's the good news: ALL your sins—past, present and future—have been forgiven! The blood of Jesus has washed them all away, and because of Jesus' perfect sacrifice at the cross, God does not keep an inventory of your sins.

Beloved, be deceived no more. ALL is forgiven! Jesus did it ONCE FOR ALL TIME. It is finished! Today, your sins cannot stop God from healing you!

Surely our sicknesses he hath borne, and our pains—he hath carried them, and we—we have esteemed him plagued, smitten of God, and afflicted. And he is pierced for our transgressions, bruised for our iniquities, the chastisement of our peace [is] on him, and by his bruise there is healing to us.

—ISAIAH 53:4–5, YLT

Bless the Lord, O my soul, and forget not all His benefits: Who forgives all your iniquities, who heals all your diseases.

—PSALM 103:2–3

Forgiveness of sins
as well as **HEALING**
are bound up in the atoning
sacrifice of Jesus.

He is still in the business of
forgiving and healing.

Receive your
forgiveness *and receive
your healing today!*

*For I will be merciful to their
unrighteousness, and their sins and their
lawless deeds I will remember no more.*

—HEBREWS 8:12

*...He adds, "Their sins and their lawless
deeds I will remember no more."*

—HEBREWS 10:17

Your Sins He Remembers No More

"Why would God heal you? Have you forgotten what you've done?"

Have such thoughts crossed your mind and discouraged you from reaching out to God for your healing? My friend, such thoughts that condemn you aren't from God or the Holy Spirit. They originate from the devil. The enemy wants you sin-conscious and will even tell you that it's "godly" to be mindful of your failures.

But God doesn't want you sin-conscious—that's *not* honoring what His Son has done for you at the cross. In fact, He declares in His Word that your sins and lawless deeds *He remembers no more*! **God's not keeping an itemized account of your sins**. So why are you?

Beloved, don't be sin-conscious today. Be Son-conscious, and watch your healing manifest!

As far as the east is from the west, so far has
He removed our transgressions from us.

—PSALM 103:12

*Can you measure
how far the East is from
the West?*

*That's **how far**
the **LORD**
has removed your
sins from you!*

As Jesus was walking along, he saw a man who had been blind from birth. "Rabbi," his disciples asked him, "why was this man born blind? Was it because of his own sins or his parents' sins?" "It was not because of his sins or his parents' sins," Jesus answered. "This happened so the power of God could be seen in him…" Then he spit on the ground, made mud with the saliva, and spread the mud over the blind man's eyes. He told him, "Go wash yourself in the pool of Siloam" (Siloam means "sent"). So the man went and washed and came back seeing!

—JOHN 9:1–7, NLT

Jesus Is Your Solution

I love how our Lord Jesus is such a loving and *practical* God. When there is a problem, He goes straight to the solution.

Before Jesus stepped in to heal the man born blind, His disciples were caught up in uncovering whose sin had made the man blind. Jesus, on the other hand, was interested only in using His power to give the poor man sight!

The same way Jesus didn't get sucked into the "blame game" is the same way He doesn't want you to. So don't ask what or whose sin caused your sickness. Forget about what you should or shouldn't have done or why it happened. Be preoccupied instead with your solution—Jesus Christ, who through the cross has removed every sin in your life and who wants to work a miracle in your body!

*There is therefore now no condemnation
for those who are in Christ Jesus.*

—ROMANS 8:1, NASB

*Who then will condemn us? No one—
for Christ Jesus died for us and was
raised to life for us, and he is sitting
in the place of honor at God's
right hand, pleading for us.*

—ROMANS 8:34, NLT

No More Condemnation

Many people are sick today because of guilt and condemnation. Condemnation kills! People condemn themselves for their sins and failures, receive condemnation from others and even think that God is condemning them to a life of sickness.

The good news of the gospel is that there is ABSOLUTELY NO condemnation for us who are in Christ, because Christ has already been condemned in our place at Calvary!

Beloved, when you reach out now and receive God's gift of no condemnation, you'll receive your healing, fully paid for by the blood of His Son!

When Jesus had raised Himself up and
saw no one but the woman, He said to
her, "Woman, where are those accusers
of yours? Has no one condemned you?"
She said, "No one, Lord." And Jesus said
to her, "Neither do I condemn you;
go and sin no more."

—JOHN 8:10–11

'No One Condemns Me'

She never expected to be caught in the act of adultery, much less be dragged to the Teacher and flung at His feet. Those who did it smugly expected Jesus to condemn her. None of them were prepared to hear Him say, "Let those who have never sinned throw the first stones!" Their consciences pricked, they left, one by one. Alone with Jesus, she heard Him say to her, "Where are your accusers? Has no one condemned you?"

Jesus knew how important it was for this woman to realize and say, "No one condemns me, Lord." The only one who *could* condemn her, *did not*, because He was going to the cross to be punished and condemned in her place.

Something happens when you know that God does not condemn you today because of the cross. The woman received the power to "go and sin (which was her problem) no more." *You* will receive the power to rise from your bed of sickness and be sick no more!

"For this is like the waters of Noah to Me; for as I have sworn that the waters of Noah would no longer cover the earth, so have I sworn that I would not be angry with you, nor rebuke you. For the mountains shall depart and the hills be removed, but My kindness shall not depart from you, nor shall My covenant of peace be removed," says the Lord, who has mercy on you.

—*ISAIAH 54:9–10*

God's Not Angry—The Rainbow In The Sky

I love rainbows. Who doesn't? But do you know how the beautiful rainbow came about?

In the Book of Genesis, God placed a beautiful rainbow in the sky to remind Himself and us of His oath never to flood the earth again. Then, in the Book of Isaiah, He declared that just as He had sworn never to flood the earth again, **He has sworn never to be angry with us again**.

My friend, God is NOT angry with you today because of the covenant of peace established by the blood of Jesus. Today, see the Lord smiling at you, eager to bless and heal you!

*When he died, he died once to break the
power of sin. But now that he lives,
he lives for the glory of God.*

—ROMANS 6:10, NLT

*For God was in Christ, reconciling the world
to himself, no longer counting people's
sins against them…*

—2 CORINTHIANS 5:19, NLT

*No power in the sky above or in the earth
below—indeed, nothing in all creation will
ever be able to separate us from the love of
God that is revealed in Christ Jesus our Lord.*

—ROMANS 8:39, NLT

Your sins are no longer an issue with God.

NOTHING

can separate you from **God's love**.

So what's there to stop you from reaching out and receiving your healing?

For He made Him who knew no sin to be sin for us, that we might become the righteousness of God in Him.

—*2 Corinthians 5:21*

He saved us, not because of righteous things we had done, but because of his mercy.

—*Titus 3:5, niv*

... the Sun of Righteousness shall arise with healing in His wings...

—*Malachi 4:2*

Not Just Forgiven, But Made Righteous Too

My friend, at the cross, Jesus did not just take away your sins, He also gave you His **righteousness**! A divine exchange took place—your sins for *His* righteousness. This means that, today, you are as righteous as Christ Himself—not because of your good works, but because of His finished work!

Place your hand over your heart right now and boldly declare:

> *I, (state your name), AM the righteousness of God in Christ!*

Come on, say it out loud at least three times and believe it in your heart every day. If the enemy tells you, "You're a bad Christian and that's why you're sick," just declare, "I AM RIGHTEOUS IN CHRIST!" When you honor the work of the Son, you'll see Him arising "with healing in His wings" for every weakness, distress and pain!

Your righteousness is an everlasting righteousness…

—PSALM 119:142

For as by one man's disobedience many were made sinners, so also by one Man's obedience many will be made righteous.

—ROMANS 5:19

David says the same thing when he speaks of the blessedness of the man to whom God credits righteousness apart from works.

—ROMANS 4:6, NIV

The Lord gives sight to the blind, the Lord lifts up those who are bowed down, the Lord loves the righteous.

—PSALM 146:8, NIV

Righteous Forever Through Christ's Obedience

Because your righteousness from the Lord is not based on what *you've* done, but what *He* has done at Calvary, you cannot lose this righteousness through the wrong that you do. And if you are righteous, healing, a blessing that belongs to the righteous, belongs to you!

When you realize that you cannot earn your righteousness, you'll realize that your failures cannot cause you to *lose* this righteousness, and therefore your right to God's healing.

Beloved, you are **forever righteous** because of JESUS' obedience (not your obedience) and finished work! Through His perfect sacrifice, He has qualified you for healing, wholeness and long life!

*For if by the one man's offense death reigned
through the one, much more those who
receive abundance of grace and of the
gift of righteousness will reign in life
through the One, Jesus Christ.*

—ROMANS 5:17

*The righteous will flourish like a palm tree,
they will grow like a cedar of Lebanon.*

—PSALM 92:12, NIV

*He does not take his eyes off the righteous;
he enthrones them with kings and
exalts them forever.*

—JOB 36:7, NIV

Those Who Know They Are Righteous Reign

Why is it so important to know and believe that you are the righteousness of God in Christ? Because it is those who know and believe that they are righteous in Christ who will *reign in life*.

When you reign in life you **reign over** sin, poverty, depression, addictions and all types of sicknesses. Having a strong and robust body is part of reigning in life. Instead of death and all its related forms reigning, life and life more abundantly will reign in you!

So every day, receive God's gift of righteousness by simply thanking Him for it, believing it in your heart and speaking it to yourself. Beloved, you can start to reign in life today!

Today I have given you the choice between life and death… Oh, that you would choose life, so that you and your descendants might live!

—DEUTERONOMY 30:19, NLT

Death and life are in the power of the tongue…

—PROVERBS 18:21

In the way of righteousness is life, and in its pathway there is no death.

—PROVERBS 12:28

And since we have the same spirit of faith, according to what is written, "I believed and therefore I spoke," we also believe and therefore speak.

—2 CORINTHIANS 4:13

Choose Life Today!

You can *choose life* today. How? By realizing that life and death are in the power of your tongue. So you can walk and reign in life every day: Instead of complaining about your symptoms, simply thank God for His gift of righteousness and declare your righteousness in Christ.

Say this prayer with me:

> *Jesus, thank You for not just loving me and removing my sins, but for also giving me Your everlasting righteousness.*
>
> *You ARE my righteousness—today, tomorrow and forevermore. And because I am righteous, I will REIGN IN LIFE through You. I will reign over sin and sickness, and live a life that glorifies You!*

*But if Christ is in you, your body is dead
because of sin, yet your spirit is alive because
of righteousness. And if the Spirit of him who
raised Jesus from the dead is living in you,
he who raised Christ from the dead will also
give life to your mortal bodies through
his Spirit, who lives in you.*

—ROMANS 8:10–11, NIV

*For it is by believing in your heart that you are
made right with God, and it is by confessing
with your mouth that you are saved.*

—ROMANS 10:10, NLT

Be Righteousness-Conscious And Receive Life

Jesus was raised from the dead by the awesome power of God's Spirit. That same death-defying, life-giving power resides in your spirit "because of righteousness"!

So the more you are conscious that you are righteous by Jesus' finished work, the more you release this divine power within you to energize your body and drive out all weakness and every disease.

That's how you allow the saving power and resurrection life of Jesus to flood and pulsate in every part of your body!

*The Lord…hears the prayers of
the righteous.*

—PROVERBS 15:29, NLT

*…The earnest prayer of a righteous
person has great power and produces
wonderful results.*

—JAMES 5:16, NLT

*Many are the afflictions of the righteous,
but the Lord delivers him out of them all.*

—PSALM 34:19

*The name of the Lord is a strong tower;
the righteous run to it and are safe.*

—PROVERBS 18:10

He Hears And Delivers You

Beloved, because of the finished work of Jesus Christ at the cross, God sees you righteous when He looks at you today.

And because you are righteous in God's sight…

God hears your prayers and delivers you out of every trouble!

For as he thinks in his heart, so is he…
—PROVERBS 23:7

Christ redeemed us from the curse of the law by becoming a curse for us, for it is written: "Cursed is everyone who is hung on a tree."

—GALATIANS 3:13, NIV

…the righteous will thrive like a green leaf.
—PROVERBS 11:28, NIV

How Do You See Yourself?

The Bible says, "As a man thinks in his heart, *so is he.*" This means that how you see yourself determines your physical health. So how do you see yourself in the midst of your symptoms, or after hearing your doctor's negative report?

Beloved, the truth is that through Jesus' finished work at the cross, you are **completely righteous** and **completely redeemed** from every curse of sickness. You are **God's beloved child** for whom Jesus did a complete work to save, heal and deliver.

So don't see yourself as the sick trying to get healed. You are *the healed, righteous and beloved child of God* facing some symptoms. Be of good cheer! There is no disease or condition that is greater than the perfect, finished work Jesus has accomplished for you. Declare what you've been made in Christ and see your body manifest this truth!

"No weapon formed against you shall prosper… This is the heritage of the servants of the Lord, and their righteousness is from Me," says the Lord.

—ISAIAH 54:17

In righteousness you shall be established; you shall be far from oppression, for you shall not fear; and from terror, for it shall not come near you.

—ISAIAH 54:14

The hope of the righteous will be gladness…

—PROVERBS 10:28

Do You Know What's Legally Yours?

Receiving healing from God is not about you begging Him for something He's already done. It's about you knowing what is already legally yours because of the cross. It's about you believing that the same way you have been righteously forgiven is the same way God has already righteously healed you.

When you have a revelation of this, once any symptom starts showing up, you will declare with faith in your heart, "NO SICKNESS in my body will prosper!" Once you are established in the right standing God has given you through Christ, fears that you may now have about not being healed will dissipate like mist under the blazing sun. And you'll see every hope you have as the righteous manifest in your body and in every area of your life!

Blessings crown the head of the righteous…

—PROVERBS 10:6, NIV

…righteousness leads to life…

—PROVERBS 11:19

…the righteous are bold as a lion.

—PROVERBS 28:1

The fruit of the righteous is a tree of life…

—PROVERBS 11:30

Believe Right And You Will Live Right

When you receive revelation of your right standing with God, everything becomes right in your life, including your physical health. This means that every organ in your body—your heart, lungs, stomach, kidneys, liver—will function correctly. You will experience divine strength, health, wholeness and life in your body.

When you know that you are right with the Lord, your mind will also be right—stable, sound and filled with peace. Depression will no longer be able to squat or linger in your mind or soul. Fears, panic attacks and phobias will evaporate and a new excitement, boldness and an expectation of good will come on you and cause you to experience the blessings that God has for you!

Beloved, I urge you to grow in the revelation that you have right standing with God!

The righteous is delivered from trouble…

—PROVERBS 11:8

The salvation of the righteous comes from the Lord; he is their stronghold in time of trouble.

—PSALM 37:39, NIV

For the Lord watches over the way of the righteous…

—PSALM 1:6, NIV

For surely, O Lord, you bless the righteous; you surround them with your favor as with a shield.

—PSALM 5:12, NIV

God's Word Is Life And Health

The Bible has a simple key to walking in life and health every day. Proverbs 4:20–22, NIV, exhorts us:

> My son, pay attention to what I say; listen closely to my words. Do not let them out of your sight, keep them within your heart; for they are life to those who find them and health to a man's whole body.

Take time today to fill your heart and renew your mind with God's promises for you, O righteous one!

Let us therefore come boldly to the throne of grace, that we may obtain mercy and find grace to help in time of need.

—HEBREWS 4:16

The righteous cry out, and the Lord hears them; he delivers them from all their troubles.

—PSALM 34:17, NIV

…the Lord upholds the righteous.

—PSALM 37:17, NIV

For the eyes of the Lord are on the righteous and his ears are attentive to their prayer.

—1 PETER 3:12, NIV

Come Boldly!

God has made you righteous through the cross of Jesus so that you can always come **boldly** into His presence and find a throne of grace—not judgment.

You need to know that God has made you righteous in His sight so that you can take up His invitation to come boldly, always expecting "to obtain mercy and find grace to help in time of need," for the littlest to the most debilitating symptom in your body.

Today, come boldly to the One who loves you passionately and unconditionally. Come boldly to the One who knows every symptom in your body and who has the healing you need. He waits eagerly for you to draw boldly from His mercy and grace!

CHAPTER 4

*See His Grace And
Be Healed*

*When she heard about Jesus, she came behind
Him in the crowd and touched His garment. For
she said, "If only I may touch His clothes, I shall
be made well." Immediately the fountain of her
blood was dried up, and she felt in her body
that she was healed of the affliction. And Jesus,
immediately knowing in Himself that power had
gone out of Him, turned around in the crowd
and said, "Who touched My clothes?"...But the
woman, fearing and trembling, knowing what
had happened to her, came and fell down before
Him and told Him the whole truth. And He said
to her, "Daughter, your faith has made you well.
Go in peace, and be healed of your affliction."*

—**MARK 5:27–34**

See Jesus' Grace And He Will See Your Faith

"I don't think I have enough faith to be healed."

My friend, it's not for you to see how much faith you have. That's God's department. All you need to do is simply see how gracious God is toward you.

The woman with the issue of blood didn't go around saying, "I must have faith. I must have faith…" No, she wasn't conscious of her faith (or lack of it). She was conscious of Jesus and His goodness. How? She heard about Jesus. She must have heard all about His kindness toward the sick and oppressed, and how He healed and delivered them ALL.

She simply saw Jesus in His grace, and Jesus saw her faith and affirmed it—"Daughter, your faith has made you well." Beloved, just focus on Jesus' grace. See how He healed ALL without qualification and keep hearing of His goodness!

153

Are you conscious of
YOUR FAITH?

Or are you conscious of
GOD'S GRACE?

See *Jesus* in
His grace,
and He will see you
in your *faith*.

Then they shall eat the flesh on that night;
roasted in fire, with unleavened bread and
with bitter herbs they shall eat it.

—EXODUS 12:8

He also brought them out with silver
and gold, and there was none feeble
among His tribes.

—PSALM 105:37

The next day John saw Jesus coming
toward him, and said, "Behold! The Lamb of
God who takes away the sin of the world!"

—JOHN 1:29

"Roasted In Fire"

They ate their way out of slavery and bondage.

God had told His people to take a lamb for each household, roast it, apply its blood on their doorposts and eat the roasted lamb in their homes that night. The next day, all the Israelites, with "none feeble" among them, walked out of Egypt into freedom.

Why eat the lamb roasted? Because it was a picture of Jesus, the true Lamb of God, exhausting the fiery wrath of God for all our sins and paying the full price for our healing at the cross.

The physical roasted lamb they ate was a shadow. Today, you have the real thing. Whenever you partake of the Holy Communion, see the true Lamb of God judged for your sins and sicknesses. He has freed and delivered you from every disease!

. . . Himself bore our sins in His own body on the tree, that we, having died to sins, might live for righteousness— by whose stripes you were healed.

—1 PETER 2:24

I am poured out like water, and all My bones are out of joint; My heart is like wax; it has melted within Me.

—PSALM 22:14

I can count all My bones. They look and stare at Me.

—PSALM 22:17

See Jesus Judged For Your Sake

To see God's grace toward us when we are sick is to see what Jesus did for us at the cross. Just as it was important for the Israelites to eat the lamb roasted before they walked free the next day, God wants you to see His provision for your healing—Jesus, the true Lamb of God—"roasted." He wants you to see Jesus SMITTEN by His judgment for your deliverance and redemption.

See Jesus carrying your symptoms and diseases on His own body. See Him taking one lash after another until His back was shredded to ribbons. See Him falling again and again under the brutality of the scourging, only to rise again and again for more beating until ALL your diseases were healed!

*Surely our griefs He Himself bore,
and our sorrows He carried.*

—ISAIAH 53:4, NASB

*But the Lord was pleased to crush
Him, putting Him to grief.*

—ISAIAH 53:10, NASB

See Jesus Smitten With Your Diseases

My wife, Wendy, broke out in hives once. The itch was so bad that she couldn't sleep for several nights, and medication didn't help much.

Her breakthrough came when she saw how much Jesus suffered for her to be well. While tossing and turning in bed one night, she pictured Jesus on the cross, smitten with her disease. She saw His hands nailed to the timber, and the Holy Spirit impressed this upon her heart: "At least you can scratch, He couldn't." Tears welled up in her eyes. By morning, she was healed!

Beloved, see His grace toward you in His willingness to bear *all* your sicknesses and pains. SURELY He has healed you!

Jesus was
judged, burnt, smitten
and crushed.

The price for
your health and wholeness
has been paid!

Is anyone among you sick? Let him call for the elders of the church, and let them pray over him, anointing him with oil in the name of the Lord. And the prayer of faith will save the sick, and the Lord will raise him up...

—JAMES 5:14–15

And being in agony, He prayed more earnestly. Then His sweat became like great drops of blood falling down to the ground.

—LUKE 22:44

But he was pierced for our transgressions, he was crushed for our iniquities; the punishment that brought us peace was upon him, and by his wounds we are healed.

—ISAIAH 53:5, NIV

...the yoke will be destroyed because of the anointing oil.

—ISAIAH 10:27

See Jesus Crushed For Your Wholeness

Why does the Bible talk about anointing the sick with oil? Is there something magical about the holy anointing oil? No, my friend. When we anoint our sick bodies with oil, we are simply releasing our faith in Jesus' finished work. He was crushed for our iniquities so that we can be made whole.

Before anointing oil can be made, olive fruit must be crushed in a press. Likewise, before healing can be dispensed to us, Jesus had to be crushed. His crushing began at Gethsemane, which means "oil press," and continued at the scourging post, ending only with His death at the cross.

Beloved, whenever you use the yoke-destroying anointing oil, see Jesus crushed for your healing. See the agony that He endured in order for His healing grace to be righteously bestowed upon you!

And Jesus, immediately knowing in Himself that power had gone out of Him, turned around in the crowd and said, "Who touched My clothes?" But His disciples said to Him, "You see the multitude thronging You, and You say, 'Who touched Me?'" And He looked around to see her who had done this thing. But the woman, fearing and trembling, knowing what had happened to her, came and fell down before Him and told Him the whole truth. And He said to her, "Daughter, your faith has made you well. Go in peace, and be healed of your affliction."

—MARK 5:30–34

Jesus Is Pleased When You Take From Him

In the healing of the woman with the issue of blood, you could say that the woman sneaked up behind Jesus and "stole" her healing! But was Jesus offended? Not at all! In fact, He was so pleased with her boldness that He just had to meet her.

Jesus did not seek her out to rebuke her. No, He sought her out so that He could affirm her with His love and assure her that He wasn't angry with her for having taken a portion of healing virtue from Him. That's why He even called her "daughter" and encouraged her to walk in her healing—"Go in peace, and be healed of your affliction."

Beloved, that's the heart of your Savior. He freely gives out His healing virtue to anyone who will take it from Him. So reach out and take from Him right now and bring pleasure to His heart!

Jesus said to him, "If you can believe, all things are possible to him who believes."

—MARK 9:23

Let us hold fast the confession of our hope without wavering, for He who promised is faithful.

—HEBREWS 10:23

O Lord of hosts, blessed is the man who trusts in You!

—PSALM 84:12

Jesus—The One Who Always Believes

Mark 9:23 has been traditionally taught to mean that you can have your miracle if YOU can believe. If you can't believe, then Jesus isn't going to give you your miracle.

But if you study the Greek structure of the verse, it's actually saying, "Can you believe that all things are possible to Him [Jesus] who is always believing?"

That makes a world of difference! It's not about how well or how much you can believe, but WHO you believe. **Jesus is the only one whose faith is always constant and never wavers**. His faith never fails! And if you can believe that all things are possible for Jesus who never doubts, never wavers, then you are on your way to receiving your miracle!

Beloved, have faith not in your faith, but in **Him** who always believes and always wants to do good to you!

Let us fix our eyes on Jesus, the author
and perfecter of our faith…
—HEBREWS 12:2, NIV

Don't focus on whether or not **you** have enough faith to be healed. **Fix your eyes** on *Jesus*, the author and perfecter of your faith!

But we all, with unveiled face, beholding as in a mirror the glory of the Lord, are being transformed into the same image from glory to glory, just as by the Spirit of the Lord.

—2 CORINTHIANS 3:18

Oh, give thanks to the Lord, for He is good! For His mercy endures forever.

—PSALM 107:1

Simply See Jesus' Goodness In The Word

I was down with a nasty fever once. I sought the Lord and He told me to simply read about His healing miracles in the Gospels. He even told me to forget doctrine and to just focus on His grace, compassion and willingness to heal the sick.

Delving into the Scriptures, I soon found myself in the presence of my healer and life-giver. I bathed in His love for me and just saw His goodness and willingness to heal me, since He healed **every person** who came to Him for healing. It wasn't long before the fever left.

Beloved, without spiritual gymnastics, but simply by seeing Jesus and His grace in the Scriptures, you can be transformed into His likeness—which includes having His resurrection life—unconsciously and effortlessly!

...He cast out the spirits with a word,
and healed all who were sick.

—MATTHEW 8:16

...great multitudes followed Him,
and He healed them all.

—MATTHEW 12:15

...the whole multitude sought to touch Him,
for power went out from Him and healed them all.

—LUKE 6:19

...God anointed Jesus of Nazareth with the
Holy Spirit and with power, who went about
doing good and healing all who were oppressed
by the devil, for God was with Him.

—ACTS 10:38

Unconditional Love And Healing

It didn't matter who they were or what kinds of past these people had. As long as they sought Him for healing, Jesus healed them gladly and graciously. He never asked them what they had done or not done, or if they had repented. He never asked them to sign a pledge to follow Him and never told anyone that He would not heal them because they deserved to be sick.

Surely none of them were perfect in their thought life or behavior. Surely there were some who came to Him without strong faith. Yet, all this didn't matter to Jesus. All that mattered to Him was that they had been suffering and needed to be set free.

Beloved, see this compassionate Savior when you come to Him for healing. He puts no demands and no conditions on you. He simply wants to heal you and set you free!

"But this is the new covenant I will make with the people of Israel on that day, says the Lord: I will put my laws in their minds, and I will write them on their hearts. I will be their God, and they will be my people. And they will not need to teach their neighbors, nor will they need to teach their relatives, saying, 'You should know the Lord.' For everyone, from the least to the greatest, will know me already. And I will forgive their wickedness, and I will never again remember their sins."

—HEBREWS 8:10–12, NLT

"I Will...I Will...I Will..."

The new covenant of grace that we are living in today is all about God saying, "I will...I will...I will..." to you. It's about **God doing** and blessing you, not you trying to earn His blessings by **your doing**.

My friend, if you come to God today and ask, "Father, will You heal me and my child despite all the wrong I've done?" He will say to you, "I WILL."

Beloved, God says to you, "I WILL heal you and your loved ones. I WILL be your God, your healer and everything you need Me to be to you." Don't try to earn your healing when Jesus has already paid for it at the cross. Instead, hear Him say, "I WILL" and see Him doing for you what you cannot do for yourself!

"I WILL...

...NO strings attached."

—Jesus

…I will bring health and healing to it;
I will heal my people and will let them
enjoy abundant peace and security.

—JEREMIAH 33:6, NIV

And my God shall supply all your need
according to His riches in glory
by Christ Jesus.

—PHILIPPIANS 4:19

The grace of our Lord Jesus Christ
be with you.

—1 CORINTHIANS 16:23

Grace That Supplies

The Lord told me once, "Being under grace means being constantly under My supply. It means being conscious not of the need, demand or crisis, but of My supply to you."

My friend, the essence of grace is supply. See yourself under His grace by seeing yourself under the waterfall of His supply. Do you need healing for your body today? See the area of affliction surrounded by His power to heal and His resurrection life!

Beloved, because of the cross, God's grace is always supplying healing, protection, wisdom and provision to you. And the more you are conscious of it, the more you will walk in it!

*Now it happened on another Sabbath,
also, that He entered the synagogue and
taught. And a man was there whose right
hand was withered...And when He had
looked around at them all, He said to
the man, "Stretch out your hand."
And he did so, and his hand was
restored as whole as the other.*

—LUKE 6:6, 10

*"The Lord is my portion," says my soul,
"Therefore I hope in Him!"*

—LAMENTATIONS 3:24

See His Supply!

It must have drawn many looks—some curious, some sympathetic, some possibly of disgust. For the owner and all who saw it, the withered hand must have spelled "challenging," "difficult" and very likely, "impossible to heal."

But where others saw the witheredness, Jesus saw only God's supply of healing and wholeness available to the man. That's why He said to him, "Stretch out your hand." Jesus didn't see the lack others saw. He only saw the Father's **superabundant supply of grace** all over that withered hand. He saw the Father's heart to heal and bless the man!

Today, don't focus on your pain, symptoms or the doctor's negative report. Whether it's an aching back, ailing heart or barren womb, see His healing power enveloping your body. See His grace supplying life and health to you!

*And this same God who takes care
of me will supply all your needs
from his glorious riches, which have
been given to us in Christ Jesus.*

—PHILIPPIANS 4:19, NLT

God's supply for you is
exceedingly,
abundantly,
above all
you can ask or think.

*Then the servants of the king of Syria said to him,
"Their gods are gods of the hills. Therefore they were
stronger than we; but if we fight against them in the
plain, surely we will be stronger than they"… Then
a man of God came and spoke to the king of Israel,
and said, "Thus says the Lord: 'Because the Syrians
have said, "The Lord is God of the hills, but He is not
God of the valleys," therefore I will deliver all
this great multitude into your hand, and you
shall know that I am the Lord.'"*

—1 KINGS 20:23, 28

*Fear not, for I am with you; be not dismayed,
for I am your God. I will strengthen you,
yes, I will help you, I will uphold you with
My righteous right hand.*

—ISAIAH 41:10

God Of The Valleys Too

In the darkest moments of our lives, we often feel like God is a thousand miles away. *God is with us on the mountaintops*, we think, *but in the valleys, we're all alone.*

Nothing could be further from the truth. In 1 Kings 20, the Syrian king was told that Syria had fought Israel on the hills and lost because Israel's God was the God of the hills. So if they fought the Israelites in the valleys, they would win. Of course, the misinformed Syrians lost again because **God is a God of the valleys too**!

My friend, there's nowhere you can go where you're not covered by God's mercy and grace. Whether you are in the pink of health or terribly ill in the valley of the shadow of death, He is with you and will never leave you nor forsake you. So don't lose hope. The God of the valleys is your strength. He will uphold you with His righteous right hand and deliver you from your enemies!

Yea, though I walk through the valley of the shadow
of death, I will fear no evil; for You are with me;
Your rod and Your staff, they comfort me.

—PSALM 23:4

For He Himself has said, "I will never
leave you nor forsake you." So we may boldly say:
"The Lord is my helper; I will not fear…"

—HEBREWS 13:5–6

He tends his flock like a shepherd:
He gathers the lambs in his arms
and carries them close to his heart…

—ISAIAH 40:11, NIV

Deliverance In The Valley

Cold. Lonely. Frightening. Abysmal. In the valley of the shadow of death, we battle with hopelessness and the fear of being abandoned.

But see how Jesus, our good shepherd, watches over and delivers us even though we walk—not by His leading—into the valley of the shadow of death. In that valley, He is still with us. He is not with us to say, "I told you so." He is not standing there, with arms folded, to see how we will get out of the trouble we got ourselves into. No, He is with us to protect and deliver us with His rod and staff from the evil one.

Beloved, Jesus is a shepherd whose tender heart toward you will never allow Him to forsake you when you need Him the most. See Him with you protecting you, delivering you from death and bringing you safely through every season of darkness.

"I will
never ever
leave you . . .

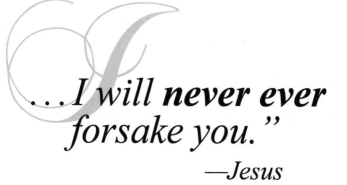

*...I will **never ever** forsake you."*

—*Jesus*

CHAPTER 5

Rest In The Finished Work

So when Jesus had received the sour wine,
He said, "It is finished!" And bowing His head,
He gave up His spirit.

—JOHN 19:30

For we who have believed do enter that rest…

—HEBREWS 4:3

There remains therefore a rest for the people
of God. For he who has entered His rest has
himself also ceased from his works as
God did from His.

—HEBREWS 4:9–10

Rest—The Work Is Finished

I've often been asked, "Pastor Prince, how do I *rest* in the finished work of Jesus so that I can receive my miracle?"

My reply is always, "See the finished work."

Beloved, when you **see and believe the finished work,** how your sins and diseases have already been nailed to or *finished* at the cross of Christ, your soul finds rest. You will no longer be troubled and agitated, trying hard to be healed because the symptoms persist, but you will be in a place of rest and faith. And when you are at rest and in faith, your healing is just around the corner!

Let us labor therefore to enter into that rest…
—HEBREWS 4:11, KJV

Let us, therefore, make every effort to enter that rest…
—HEBREWS 4:11, NIV

Be anxious for nothing, but in everything by prayer and supplication, with thanksgiving, let your requests be made known to God; and the peace of God, which surpasses all understanding, will guard your hearts and minds through Christ Jesus.
—PHILIPPIANS 4:6–7

Labor To Enter Into Rest

"Don't just stand there, do something!"

Our human tendency is to worry and fear, and to try all sorts of methods to solve the problem at hand. We find it very hard to just trust the Lord and rest in His finished work.

That's why the Bible says that we are to **labor** to enter His rest. This sounds like an oxymoron, doesn't it? But the truth is that it takes some "laboring" on our part to be restful.

Beloved, instead of making every effort to be healed, the Lord wants us to make every effort to be at rest!

Don't get into
self-effort
to earn your healing.

Make every effort
to be at *rest*.

However, when He, the Spirit of truth, has come, He will guide you into all truth…

—JOHN 16:13

For those who live according to the flesh set their minds on the things of the flesh, but those who live according to the Spirit, the things of the Spirit. For to be carnally minded is death, but to be spiritually minded is life and peace.

—ROMANS 8:5–6

Rest Is Spirit-Directed Activity

Resting in the finished work of Jesus is not inactivity or laziness. Rest will always result in Holy Spirit-directed activity.

While you are trusting God for your healing, you may need specific wisdom to deal practically with your physical symptoms. This comes from the Holy Spirit. He wants to guide you into all truth and lead you to victory.

For example, if you have a stomach ulcer, He may tell you, "Stop that stressful activity," or "Spend more time playing with your kids." You see, He knows exactly what the problem is and has the perfect solution that will bring about the results you desire!

Beloved, if you live by the Spirit and follow His promptings, you will find life, peace and victory!

And if by grace, then it is no longer of works;
otherwise grace is no longer grace.
But if it is of works, it is no longer grace;
otherwise work is no longer work.

—ROMANS 11:6

Act Out Of Rest

Whether it is partaking of the Holy Communion or confessing God's Word, do these things out of rest. Don't feel as if you need to put the demand on yourself to be healed. My friend, you can't earn your healing. It is something that God gives you by His grace.

Beloved, God wants you to see that Jesus has already paid for your healing. Today, He is so pleased with Jesus' finished work that **He is more than happy to bountifully supply** all the healing (and more!) that you desire.

When you truly have a revelation of this, nothing will stop you from declaring His Word over yourself and running to the Lord's table with thanksgiving and expectation. And when you act in faith out of rest, it won't be long before you see your miracle manifest!

*…Jesus said, "Come to me, all of you
who are weary and carry heavy burdens,
and I will give you rest."*
—MATTHEW 11:28, NLT

Peace I leave with you, My peace I give to you…
—JOHN 14:27

*But those who wait on the Lord
shall renew their strength; they shall mount up
with wings like eagles, they shall run and not be
weary, they shall walk and not faint.*

—ISAIAH 40:31

Jesus Gives You Rest

You don't need to be a Bible scholar or theologian to understand rest. You just need to be someone who knows Jesus, because it is *Jesus* who gives you rest!

My friend, if you are weary, confused and tired because of all your efforts to get healed, just go to Him right now and tell Him, "Jesus, I'm so tired and confused. I'm scared too. Please hold me in Your arms and give me rest."

You don't have to say anything if you don't want to. You can just cry in His presence. Beloved, He already knows all that you are going through. And the One who bottles your tears will surely rest you and give you peace. He will lift you up and strengthen you!

"*Come to Me…*

...I will give you *rest.*"

—Jesus

*Then she said, "Sit still, my daughter, until you know
how the matter will turn out; for the man will not rest
until he has concluded the matter this day."*

—RUTH 3:18

*...He is the faithful God who keeps his covenant
for a thousand generations...*

—DEUTERONOMY 7:9, NLT

*...I know the one in whom I trust,
and I am sure that he is able to guard
what I have entrusted to him...*

—2 TIMOTHY 1:12, NLT

When You Rest, He Works

The Old Testament story of Ruth is a love story I love to preach about. Ruth was a poor, Gentile widow, who ended up marrying Boaz, a wealthy, honorable relative who was willing to redeem her from her pitiful life.

In the story, there is a scene where Ruth is told by Naomi, her mother-in-law, to "sit still," for she knew Boaz was someone who would not rest until he concluded the matter of redeeming Ruth that day.

My friend, when you "sit still" in the face of persistent symptoms, Jesus, your willing and able kinsman Redeemer, goes to work on your behalf. And *He* will not rest until your case is settled. So rest from your self-efforts, and allow Jesus to work on your case!

Be still, and know that I am God.

—PSALM 46:10

Be still.

Let go and let God be God to you.
Let Him give you your healing miracle.

... Let not your heart be troubled,
neither let it be afraid.

—JOHN 14:27

Above all else, guard your heart, for it is
the wellspring of life.

—PROVERBS 4:23, NIV

Guard your heart above all else, for it
determines the course of your life.

—PROVERBS 4:23 NLT

A tranquil heart is life to the body...

—PROVERBS 14:30, NASB

Guard Your Heart

The Bible tells us that the heart is where the issues of life spring forth. What we allow to enter our hearts will affect our thoughts, actions and even our bodies. In other words, the condition of one's heart determines the course of one's life!

That is why Jesus, who bequeathed to us His peace, tells us, "Let not your heart be troubled, neither let it be afraid." So if we want to walk in His peace and rest, we need to guard our hearts and not let them spiral into negative thoughts, worry and fear. The Book of Wisdom also tells us that a peaceful and cheerful heart promotes health.

Beloved, there may be many things in our lives that we want to "guard," such as our health or careers, but God wants us to guard our hearts above all else, and **He will guard the rest**!

A merry heart
does good, like…

...MEDICINE.

—PROVERBS 17:22

...when evening had come, He said to them, "Let us cross over to the other side." Now when they had left the multitude, they took Him along in the boat as He was... And a great windstorm arose, and the waves beat into the boat, so that it was already filling. But He was in the stern, asleep on a pillow. And they awoke Him and said to Him, "Teacher, do You not care that we are perishing?" Then He arose and rebuked the wind, and said to the sea, "Peace, be still!" And the wind ceased and there was a great calm.

—MARK 4:35–39

The Prince Of Peace Is With You

Panic filled the storm-tossed boat as icy water crashed in. Within minutes, the disciples were screaming over the howling winds, "Jesus, don't you care? We're drowning!"

Sound asleep in the boat, the Prince of Peace awoke and rose to His feet at the cry of His disciples. Unfazed by the wind and waves, He pointed to the storm and said, "Peace, be still!" Immediately, the turbulent waters became as smooth as glass.

Beloved, if you're grappling with a challenging condition in your body right now, take heart. The Prince of Peace resides in you. You are NOT going under, but going OVER! When you feel overwhelmed, just cry out to Him. Let His peace flood first your heart, then every part of your body!

Then He arose and rebuked the wind, and said to the sea, "Peace, be still!" And the wind ceased and there was a great calm. But He said to them, "Why are you so fearful? How is it that you have no faith?"

—**MARK 4:39-40**

You will keep him in perfect peace, whose mind is stayed on You, because he trusts in You.

—**ISAIAH 26:3**

Give all your worries and cares to God, for he cares about you.

—**1 PETER 5:7, NLT**

Kept In Perfect Peace

I believe that one reason Jesus could calm the storm in this much-loved story was that He was the only one in the boat who was at peace. And what was within Him overflowed and affected the storm outside.

After Jesus had stilled the storm for His disciples, He corrected them for letting their hearts be troubled. And in His loving rebuke, He shows us how we can always have peace in our hearts. "Why are you so fearful?" He asked them. "How is it that you have no faith?" In other words, "Why do you take so little from Me?"

Beloved, God loves you dearly and wants to supply you with His health and healing. When you know and believe this, fear will flee and peace will rule in your heart.

Because **Jesus**, *the*
Prince of Peace,
is in your boat…

...*the only thing that*
is **going under**
is your sickness and pain!

*For with stammering lips and another
tongue He will speak to this people, to
whom He said, "This is the rest with
which You may cause the weary to
rest," and, "This is the refreshing"…*

—ISAIAH 28:11–12

*…He said, "My Presence will go with
you, and I will give you rest."*

—EXODUS 33:14

The Holy Spirit's Rest And Refreshing

You've probably heard of the term "R&R." It's commonly used in the military and it means "rest and relaxation" after some exhausting overseas training or mission. Doctors also order "rest and rehabilitation" for the injured and sick.

My friend, God has an R&R for you too. It's called "the rest and the refreshing," and it comes through praying in the Holy Spirit or tongues.

One of the best ways to rest and be refreshed, especially when you are worried, fatigued or just waiting for the manifestation of your healing, is to pray in the Holy Spirit.

Beloved, give yourself some time every day to pray in the Spirit, and allow Him to rejuvenate and refresh you supernaturally!

*And the Holy Spirit helps us in our weakness.
For example, we don't know what God wants
us to pray for. But the Holy Spirit prays for
us with groanings that cannot be expressed
in words. And the Father who knows all
hearts knows what the Spirit is saying, for
the Spirit pleads for us believers in harmony
with God's own will. And we know that God
causes everything to work together for the
good of those who love God and are called
according to his purpose for them.*

—ROMANS 8:26–28, NLT

Let The Holy Spirit Intercede For You

Sometimes, when our healing is not forthcoming, we just don't know what else to pray. We've prayed from every angle we know how, using all the scriptures we know of, and yet, there doesn't seem to be any breakthrough.

I want you to know that God has given us a weapon that will break down every barrier—praying in tongues. When you don't know what to pray, pray in the Holy Spirit and allow Him to intercede for you. He knows exactly what the problem is and what the best solution is. He will not just plead for you in harmony with God's will, but He will also rest your weary soul!

My friend, allow the Holy Spirit to intercede for you, and see God cause *everything* to work together for the good of your body and health!

Take *TIME OUT* today
to be refreshed and
rejuvenated.

Pray in the Spirit. Experience

REST &
REFRESHING,

Holy Ghost style.

By faith Sarah herself also received strength to conceive seed, and she bore a child when she was past the age, because she judged Him faithful who had promised.

—HEBREWS 11:11

If we are faithless, He remains faithful; He cannot deny Himself.

—2 TIMOTHY 2:13

...I am alert and active, watching over My word to perform it.

—JEREMIAH 1:12, AMP

Judge God Faithful

We often hear about Abraham's faith, but do you know that his wife, Sarah, had faith too? She received divine strength to conceive Isaac, even though by this time, as a woman who had never conceived, she was doubly barren!

How did Sarah find faith? The Bible tells us that she "judged Him faithful who had promised." She was conscious of *the Lord's faithfulness*, not her own faithfulness!

My friend, rest in the faithfulness of Jesus. It's not your faith but His faithfulness—His faithfulness in always loving you and making good on His promise to heal you. When you find yourself wavering in faith, judge Him faithful and be at rest. He cannot fail you and will do as His Word has promised!

Then the Lord told him, "I am the Lord who brought you out of Ur of the Chaldeans to give you this land as your possession." But Abram replied, "O Sovereign Lord, how can I be sure that I will actually possess it?"...So the Lord made a covenant with Abram that day and said, "I have given this land to your descendants, all the way from the border of Egypt to the great Euphrates River..."
—GENESIS 15:7–8, 18, NLT

My covenant I will not break, nor alter the word that has gone out of My lips.
—PSALM 89:34

...Jesus has become the guarantee of a better covenant.
—HEBREWS 7:22, NIV

Our Covenant-Keeping God

When God promised to give Abraham land, Abraham asked, "God, how can I be sure?" And as if His word wasn't good enough, God went one step further and cut a **covenant** with Abraham, binding Himself irrevocably to it to reassure His friend that He would do as promised.

Let me say something about God's covenants. They can *never* be broken, only replaced with a better one. My friend, God will do as He has promised you, and to set your heart at ease, He bound Himself to a **covenant** with you when He cut it with your representative, Jesus, at Calvary.

So rest easy in the knowledge that you have a covenant-keeping God who CANNOT break His covenant or renege on His promises. Simply lean on HIS faithfulness and like Abraham, you will walk in your inheritance and healing.

When we are *faithless*...

...He remains
faithful.

Rest in
His faithfulness
to heal you.

The Lord said to my Lord, "Sit at My right hand," till I make Your enemies Your footstool."

—MATTHEW 22:44

For He must reign till He has put all enemies under His feet. The last enemy that will be destroyed is death.

—1 CORINTHIANS 15:25–26

For he raised us from the dead along with Christ and seated us with him in the heavenly realms because we are united with Christ Jesus.

—EPHESIANS 2:6, NLT

Remain Seated With Christ

In some ancient battles, the conquered would be placed one by one under the feet of the victorious king. Likewise, in God's kingdom, Jesus has defeated all His enemies at Calvary, and God is now placing every one of them under His feet, the last being death.

The Bible says that we are seated with Christ—a position of rest. And as you rest with Christ, God will place every one of your enemies—every symptom, every disease—under your feet!

Many of us want our diseases to be under our feet first, before we will rest. But God wants us to rest first, and then HE will place every disease under our feet!

Jesus also said, "The Kingdom of God is like a farmer who scatters seed on the ground. Night and day, while he's asleep or awake, the seed sprouts and grows, but he does not understand how it happens. The earth produces the crops on its own. First a leaf blade pushes through, then the heads of wheat are formed, and finally the grain ripens."

—MARK 4:26–28, NLT

Still other seeds fell on fertile soil, and they sprouted, grew, and produced a crop that was thirty, sixty, and even a hundred times as much as had been planted!

—MARK 4:8, NLT

Toward The Hundredfold

First the blade, then the head, and then the full grain in the head of wheat. Just as a seed takes time to sprout and grow, it may take some time before your healing manifests fully. And just as a new farmer may see a thirty or sixtyfold yield before he sees a hundredfold yield, it may take some time before you experience 100 percent wholeness.

My friend, don't say, "Why is my healing taking so long?" and give up. Press on toward the hundredfold. As you get 30 percent better, trust God for the 60 percent, and then the 100 percent.

Don't lose sleep over when or how the full manifestation of your healing will happen. Be like the farmer—go to sleep! Rest, and leave the how and when to God. Beloved, the Lord will give you strength to persevere. Your hundredfold is on the way!

Every day they continued to meet together in the temple courts. They broke bread in their homes and ate together with glad and sincere hearts.

—ACTS 2:46, NIV

The true bread of God is the one who comes down from heaven and gives life to the world.

—JOHN 6:33, NLT

Then Jesus declared, "I am the bread of life. He who comes to me will never go hungry, and he who believes in me will never be thirsty."

—JOHN 6:35, NIV

…as your days, so shall your strength be.

—DEUTERONOMY 33:25

Continue In God's Grace

I thank God for the Holy Communion because each time you partake, you get to ingest and manifest more and more of Jesus' life and strength.

Beloved, keep on taking Communion until you are completely healed. As you do, thank God that you *are already healed* by Jesus' stripes. When you drink the cup, see how Jesus *has already taken away* every sin and redeemed you from sickness. See the work as **finished** and be at **rest**, knowing that you are **seated** with Christ.

Remember that it's all about what our Lord Jesus has done. **It's all His grace**, His undeserved, unmerited favor toward you. As you partake, see Jesus, the bread of life working on the inside of you, making you stronger and stronger each day!

Therefore we also, since we are surrounded by so great a cloud of witnesses, let us lay aside every weight…and let us run with endurance the race that is set before us, looking unto Jesus, the author and finisher of our faith, who for the joy that was set before Him endured the cross, despising the shame, and has sat down at the right hand of the throne of God.

—HEBREWS 12:1–2

"Behold, all those who were incensed against you shall be ashamed and disgraced; they shall be as nothing, and those who strive with you shall perish. You shall seek them and not find them—those who contended with you. Those who war against you shall be as nothing, as a nonexistent thing. For I, the Lord your God, will hold your right hand, saying to you, 'Fear not, I will help you.'"

—ISAIAH 41:11–13

DON'T GIVE UP.
*Heaven is cheering
you on—*your
healing
is just around the corner!

Prayers

Salvation Prayer

If you would like to receive all that Jesus has done for you and make Him your Lord and Savior, please pray this prayer:

Lord Jesus, thank You for loving me and dying for me on the cross. Your precious blood washes me clean of every sin. You are my Lord and Savior, now and forever. I believe that You rose from the dead and that You are alive today. Because of Your finished work, I am now a beloved child of God and heaven is my home. Thank You for giving me eternal life and filling my heart with Your peace and joy. Amen.

⟨ℐ⟩

Holy Communion Prayer

As you partake of the Holy Communion, keep seeing and declaring how you have been healed by Jesus' stripes, and how His blood has washed away all your sins and qualified you to receive His healing and health.

Hold the bread in your hand and say this:

Thank You, Jesus, for Your broken body. Thank You for bearing my symptoms and sicknesses at the cross so that I may have Your health and wholeness. I declare that by Your stripes, by the beatings You bore, by the lashes which fell on Your back, I am completely healed. I believe and I receive Your resurrection life in my body today. (Eat the bread.)

Next, take the cup in your hand and say this:

Thank You, Jesus, for Your blood that has washed me whiter than snow. Your blood has brought me forgiveness and made me righteous forever. And as I drink, I celebrate and partake of the inheritance of the righteous, which includes preservation, healing, wholeness and all Your blessings. (Drink the wine.)

Thank You, Jesus. I love You because You first loved me.

Anointing Oil Prayer

You may approach a pastor or leader in church to pray over and consecrate your oil for you. As a king and priest in Christ (Revelation 1:6), you can also pray over the oil and set it apart to be holy. Here's a prayer for blessing and sanctifying your oil:

In the name of Jesus, I set this oil apart to be holy anointing oil.

Jesus, I thank You that You were crushed for my complete healing and wholeness. This holy anointing oil speaks of the perfection of Your finished work. I thank You that whatever this oil touches, the fullness of Your grace, power and healing virtue will flow, according to Your Word in Mark 6:13 and James 5:14.

I pray that wherever this oil is applied, it will bring glory and praise to Your name. Amen.

We Would Like To Hear From You

If you have prayed the salvation prayer, or if you have a healing testimony to share after reading this book, please send us an email at info@josephprince.com

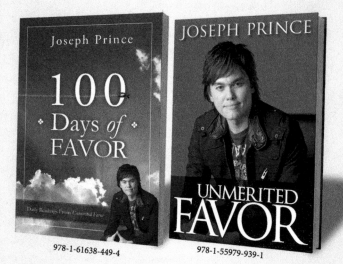